Love at First Sight

by
Cindy Hedrick

Love at First Sight
by Cindy Hedrick

Copyright © 2021

All rights reserved.

In accordance with the U.S. Copyright Act of 1976, the scanning, uploading and electronic sharing of any part of this book without the permission of the publisher is unlawful piracy and theft of the author's intellectual property. If you would like to use material from the book (other than for review purposes), prior written permission must be obtained by contacting the publisher.

Photographs from the author's personal collection.

ISBN 978-1-9550-95-04-4

Published in the United States by
CLASS LLC
Publishing Division
P.O. Box 2884
Pawleys Island, SC 29585
www.ClassAtPawleys.com

*It is man's sympathy with all creatures that first makes him truly a man.
Until he extends his circle of compassion to all living things, man will not himself find peace.*

*Dr. Albert Schweitzer
Nobel Peace Prize, 1952*

Ashley helping with fundraising and awareness at a festival in Charlotte.

Dedication

In my dedication for *Tails from SC CARES*, I astonishingly omitted a vital person who has truly been with me through "ALL" of this – my wonderful daughter, Ashley Hedrick. When she was approximately 8 years old, I took Ashley with me on animal cruelty cases, and I know it was not the best thing I did as a mom! She would help me with the animals we were forced to confiscate and was a huge help not only to me but also to those animals! Another thing that will not get me the "mother of the year" award, was letting her climb a small square fenced enclosure that had no door to help

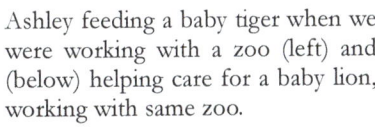
Ashley feeding a baby tiger when we were working with a zoo (left) and (below) helping care for a baby lion, working with same zoo.

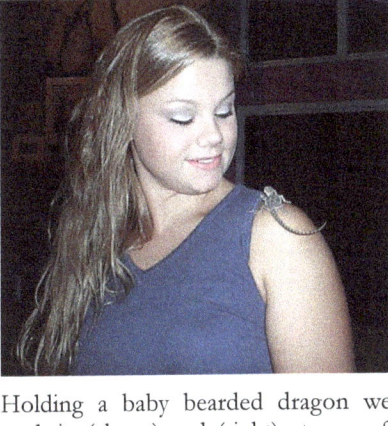
Holding a baby bearded dragon we took in (above) and (right) at one of the SC CARES festivals, helping the last tortoise across the finish line so he is not left out!

Dedication

lift out a starving pup that had no food, no water, and no shelter! Ashley was a champ, climbing in and lifting the dog up so I could get him, then climbing back out! It was not the best thing for a mom to do, but the starving pup was so happy we did – it saved his life!

Throughout all of Ashley's childhood there were animals, mostly dogs, cats and at one point a horse we saved from the glue factory that lived in our backyard. Unlike other children with chores of housework, yardwork, Ashley's chores involved poop! Helping me feed and clean up after animals was a part of her life. The one part I do not think she minded as much, was loving on them! As Ashley prepared to go to college we had taken in exotics, so her weekends at home were filled with helping the animals once again!

Even as an adult, while married to a wonderful husband, having her own family, and raising three beautiful children, she continued to help from four hours away, serving as a board member for SC CARES. She would come up with ideas, plans, and solutions. My co-rescuer for so many years, my biggest supporter both physically and mentally! She listened to me cry and has given me words of comfort; she listened to my worries and fears and helped ease my mind; always encouraging me and coming up with ideas to make things better. My child, my partner in animal rescue and my best friend for life, I love you, Ashley!

Helping prep for one of our festivals at the sanctuary and doing two of the hardest jobs, especially cleaning the rabbit room!

Giving Snuggles some love! This is the parrot I used to put in her bed to try to get her up, but it did not work! I would go back and the two of them were snuggled up under the covers!

I also dedicate these stories to anyone who might read them, and my wish is that the readers are able to open their hearts and minds to being compassionate for all creatures and our earth that we all share. To my grandchildren, Emma, James, and John, I love you with all my heart!

Lastly, she is teaching all her children to love and respect animals!

Chapters

Foreword		1
1	A Love Story	3
2	The Biggest Loser	8
3	A Rooster's Life is Very Busy!	13
4	Batman	19
5	Gracie, the Sugar Glider	26
6	Two Cows, One Moo	30
7	Monte – Please Don't Skip This Story	39
8	Kumar	45
9	Pickles & Handsome, Demolition Duo	52
10	A Mother and Son	58
11	Chester, the One-Eyed Owl	64
12	The Sweetest Family Ever	70
Afterword		77
Words and their Definitions		80
Sanctuaries and Acknowledgment		82

"So, you think you want an animal companion?"

If you feel it in your heart to share your life with any animal, please do your research before you take on this responsibility. The biggest reason that companionship with these animals fails is because people are not educated in what to expect in living with them.

Here are some suggestions as to what you need to know:

How long does this animal normally live?
What is the proper diet for this animal?
What the best housing for this animal?
How close is the nearest veterinarian for the animal?
What type of enrichment (play) does the animal need?
How is having this animal going to impact my life?

Most importantly, am I going to be able to provide all these things for this animal and keep it for its entire lifetime?

Foreword

If you have read *Tails from SC CARES*, then you know the extended version of how it all began, but if not, you should read it! There are more stories of amazing animals! This is the short version: Skip Yeager, my husband and partner in this endeavor, took wildlife rehabilitation classes with me, which then led us into rescuing exotics animals! Little did we know we would end up selling all that we had and opening a sanctuary for exotic, farm, and non-releasable wildlife!

Our sanctuary, called SC CARES, was in operation for 13 years and allowed us to help hundreds of animals of all types find happiness, be cared for, and most importantly feel loved and that they mattered! Then tragedy struck and we found out Skip had cancer. Now moreover it was still such a struggle to find funding, help, and the worry and stress of it all just became too much for me to bear. I feared the possible negative impact it all might have for the animals' lives. We then successfully placed the 150 animal residents we had in other wonderful sanctuaries in a truly short 11-month period and dissolved SC CARES.

In the process of publishing "Tails," I found out that I, too, have cancer, so I must admit that our Creator knew what was coming, and I am sure helped us make a way for the animals to continue to thrive elsewhere. In dealing with the heartache I feel from missing the animals, I discovered I also missed sharing their stories, which led me to the books I have been writing! I hope you enjoy their stories, that you understand animals are sentient creatures, with likes and dislikes, moods and feelings, and special knowledge that helps them survive. Finally, I hope you will feel compassion in your heart for them!

Sincerely and, as always, for the animals!
Cindy Hedrick & Skip Yeager,
Founders and Directors of SC CARES

Meet Charlie at 12!

1
A Love Story

At SC CARES, we had more than 50 parrot residents of various species. In 2004, we were working with a wildlife group called WRI in Winston Salem, NC. Many of the wildlife rehabilitators had taken in exotics that we received calls for, and with nowhere to turn, these animals would be put down. This is where the concept for SC CARES originated. We saw a need and made a way. We had taken in a male umbrella cockatoo named Charlie from the president of the WRI group. At the time Charlie was 12 years old and just as sweet as you can imagine. I trusted him so much that I would take him out, and we would take naps together on the couch.

In the beginning stages of SC CARES, we were living in North Carolina and thought that adopting these creatures out might be worth a try. Charlie was our first adoption. Some acquaintances of ours had expressed an interest in having Charlie live with them – so we gave it a shot. He was adopted out and moved to Vermont. Sadly, after less than a year of living with a parrot and the fact that Charlie bit the teenage boy of the home, we received a call that Charlie was returning to us. They could no longer deal with the noise and the mess, and the bite was the last straw. Charlie was back with us again and had to adjust to all the changes he had been through. Parrots do not deal with change very well; even the slightest change in their lives, such as relocating their cage to a different area, can create traumatic effects on them. Putting Charlie through all of this made us very reluctant to adopt animals out, with the fear this could happen again.

Meanwhile, after five years of searching for the right place to open SC CARES, we discovered the property we are on in Georgetown, SC, and started the moving process with 36 animals we had already taken in. Two years after opening SC CARES, we received a call from our previous WRI president that she was downsizing to work with dog rescue. She asked if we would be able to take several parrots that she had rescued. Luckily, at the time we had room, so we said yes! When she arrived with the birds, she brought another umbrella cockatoo named Stormy. Stormy's paperwork stated that she was an elder parrot at 62 years of age. Stormy had several homes and

Meet Stormy at 62.

Stormy loved shower time!

A Love Story

all those changes really took their toll on her. She began to pluck her feathers out because she was so nervous, like humans that bite their nails or, in extreme cases, pull their hair out when they are nervous or upset. If a parrot has pulled their feathers out for a long time, the follicles will close, and no more new feathers will come back. It's a sad thing that she was so upset that she would do this, but it just goes to show that parrots should not be in captivity but, instead, free in the wild. In the case of cockatoos, they would live in Australia.

Back to the reunion. We got the birds settled in and, right away, Stormy and Charlie connected. It was as if they were long-lost friends! The WRI president realized that they had been together previously at her house

Preening each other (which means to straighten and clean the feathers) is something couples do.

before we took Charlie. These two had been together several years at her house, then separated for at least five years, but in just seconds, they recognized each other and were SO thrilled to be together again. Wow – what a reunion it was for them! Parrots do not forget; sometimes that is a good thing, other times not so much.

Every day at SC CARES the birds were out of their houses after they were fed, and never a day went by that Charlie and Stormy were not snuggled together during their time out. Their houses are side by side, so they do not feel alone when they go to bed each night. What sweet birds, and what a romance – a now 67-year-old female and a 16-year-old male – in love with each other every day! It just goes to show us that humans are not the only ones who know what love is!

Jimmy when he arrived in 2008.

2
The Biggest Loser

This is a story about a sweet, gentle pig named Jimmy, a Vietnamese pot belly pig who arrived at SC CARES in 2008. The people who called and asked us to take him in thought it was funny that he was so large. The guy who brought him was even laughing because Jimmy could not walk on his own, and let me tell you, it took ALL that I had to keep my anger from exploding on him! When he arrived, Jimmy had to be hoisted from the back of a pickup truck in a blanket, unable to walk due his huge size, overgrown hooves, and the fact that he was blind. These people had named him Jimmy Dean and thought that was funny, but for us, it was just disrespectful and mean, so we called him Jimmy or JD. This pitiful creature was mortally terrified, to put it mildly. At the young age of 4, Jimmy had spent the past two years of his life locked in the laundry room of a mobile home, living in his own excrement. This was a horrible life for him because pigs, believe it or not, are exceptionally clean creatures! All those years, Jimmy was unable to get outside, walk around or do anything that pigs like to do. He had been fed primarily dog food and was given candy and gum for treats. This was a tragedy for Jimmy, since dog food did not supply him with the nutrition he needed. It only gave him fat, in addition to the candy and gum which pigs should NEVER have! He gained so much weight, so fast, that his eyelids were too heavy to open. The fat that weighed them down made it impossible for him to blink, causing his eyes to essentially dry up, leaving him blind for life.

Jimmy's front hooves when he arrived – animal cruelty at its worst!

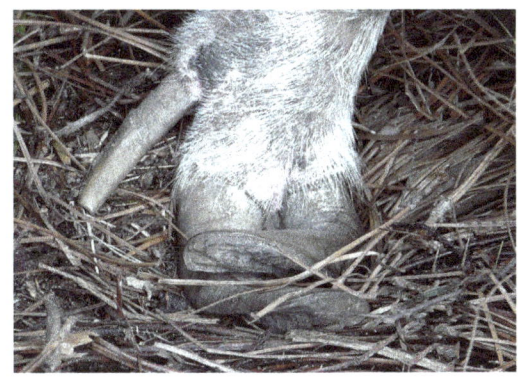

When Jimmy arrived, we began our treatment plan to do all that we could to help

The Biggest Loser

this big fellow have a happy life. His hooves took several trimmings before they were back to a normal length, and we started him on a pig pellet diet along with veggies and a little fruit. After being examined by the vet, it was determined that Jimmy's sight would never return. Even once he lost weight, his eyes were no longer functional. Thankfully, pigs have a strong sense of smell, and because of this, Jimmy was able to find his food bowl even though he could not see it! We used a mathematical calculation based on length and girth to determine weight for our pigs, and Jimmy came to us weighing 351 pounds! His entire belly rubbed the ground as he moved, and his little feet could barely get him up. A pig of his build should not weigh more than 200 to 225 pounds, so we had our work cut out for us!

In 2009, we took in an infant feral pig named Daisy.

Jimmy four years later less 75 pounds. Finally, some light under that belly!

Daisy was not only Jimmy's roommate but also his personal trainer. She would, at times, attempt to get him to play with her, which at least got him up and moving around, giving him some exercise which he desperately needed. This is not to say that he enjoyed it, as he grunted in protest. Over a four-year period, Jimmy had lost 75 pounds and weighed 276, which still left him overweight. Animals like people can get arthritis as they age and being overweight would almost certainly guarantee this would be an issue. We started Jimmy on glucosamine to help him as he aged. Jimmy's life was now filled with the proper foods, medications, friendship, and all the love he could stand!

Here are some interesting pig facts for you:

First, pigs cannot sweat! They do not have sweat glands and cannot pant like our canine friends, so they tend to suffer from heat exhaustion if they cannot find other ways to cool themselves. This is why they love mud holes! The mud not only cools their bodies but will

Best friends enjoying a bath together!

also coat their skin to help keep bugs from biting them. Humans will pay lots of money for mud baths, and the pigs already knew how great it was!

Second, pigs are highly intelligent creatures, listed number 4 in intelligence tests behind chimpanzees, dolphins, and elephants.

Third, pigs are very social creatures and enjoy the bonds they form with each other and other species.

Fourth, pigs use grunts to communicate with each other and, of course, an occasional loud squeal if they become frightened or are unhappy about something.

Fifth, a pig's snout is a sensitive organ, giving them not only a great gift of smell but also strong enough to dig up roots from the earth.

Sixth, a pig's tail wags just like a dog's when they are excited or happy, which is usually when they know the food is coming! Jimmy's tail would sway back and forth the ENTIRE time he was eating.

I cannot tell a lie; pigs do LOVE to eat!

Jimmy snoozing which is his second favorite thing to do, besides eating!

Simon singing his morning song!

3
A Rooster's Life is Very Busy

In this story, you will meet a rooster named Simon, a gamecock, who really has a very busy life! Simon, like all roosters, starts the day by singing! His song is the wake-up alarm for the hens he lives with and anyone else who is within listening distance! Simon wakes up singing every day, whether it is to the sunshine or the clouds of a yucky day, he is simply happy that he has a new day! We could probably all learn something from the roosters, and be grateful we, too, have another day!

After several minutes of his song, the day has come alive, and the hens are out looking for breakfast, so Simon starts helping them search. He scratches around trying to find bugs for them to eat and, surprisingly, gives

Simon looking for bugs!

Simon and one of his hens.

Isn't she lovely!
Her name is Mabel!

them all to the hens! When he successfully uncovers a morsel, he stands over it, guarding it while he calls to the hens to come and get it! Isn't that just the sweetest thing you have ever heard? I am sure he eats, too, otherwise he would not be healthy, but I do believe he shares most of his treasures with the girls. In captivity, such as at SC CARES, the chickens are given a scratch mix to eat in addition to treats such as grapes, watermelon, and lettuce! All of them love the treats, and we love that they eat them, since those items help keep them hydrated and healthy!

Time for our lettuce treat!

The entire time the girls are eating, Simon helps them search, but most importantly he stands guard! He is the protector of the flock and must watch for any danger to alert them and keep them safe. He is constantly looking around, up, down, across his landscape and is always aware of his surroundings! If anything were to threaten his flock, Simon would fight to his death, if needed, to protect them. He really loves and cares for the hens. At times, some of the hens will separate off into smaller groups, and for Simon, this is very annoying! If they get too far apart, he cannot watch over them all at once, so he will go to one of the groups and spreading his wings open and talking to them, he manages to gather them back together.

On warm sunny days, in the afternoon, the hens will often take a dust bath! Yes, they bathe in dirt! The chicken's skin has pores that produce oil, so if they do not dust bathe, their skin and feathers become oily and all the feathers stick together. To stay healthy, they must keep their feathers smooth and silky. The hens will find a patch of dirt and scratch through it until they have a nice pile of fresh, loose dirt. Then they will lay on one side, and using their feet, they toss the dirt onto their bodies. It is a funny site to watch, the hen on her side with dirt flying up in the air all around her in a dusty cloud! Of course, they take turns but sometimes when the sun is warm, it feels so good to them that they fall asleep! I cannot tell you how many volunteers came to me saying, "I

One of the hens taking her dust bath!

Some chickens love human hugs like Henny Penny!

think one of the chickens is dead" and I would simply ask if they were laying in pile of dirt. If the answer was "yes," then I knew exactly what was happening!

We are now into late afternoon and it is time for supper, so the whole routine of eating starts again, not that it ever actually stopped. After supper, when the

Hey girls, I found one but it's under the freezer…

A Rooster's Life

sun starts going down, Simon begins to gather all the girls to go to the coop, so they can go to bed. There are days that it seems to take a while, and I feel certain Simon is very tired and so relieved when they all go to sleep. This means "he" can finally rest after such a busy day. I can bet that Simon sleeps with one eye open, though, since he is still on guard over the hens, but he must get some rest since tomorrow is a new day and his entire routine starts all over again!

My hope is this story gives you some insight into what it would be like to be a rooster, and that you might think about how animals are a lot like us! They care for each other, like to eat and take a bath, and love their families just like we do!

Simon looking majestic.

Batman and friend, Robin, when they were rescued.

4
Batman

SC CARES focused on exotic, farm, and non-releasable wildlife rescue, but occasionally canines ended up with us from critical situations. It was a cold, rainy day in March 2013, when we received a call that two dogs were found in a field near SC CARES, and one of the dogs could not even get up. Two wonderful saviors pulled up to the sanctuary in a nice car and opened the back door where two muddy, wet dogs were. The sight of them took my breath! These poor dogs were both terribly emaciated, and one of the

These two souls knew we would help them.

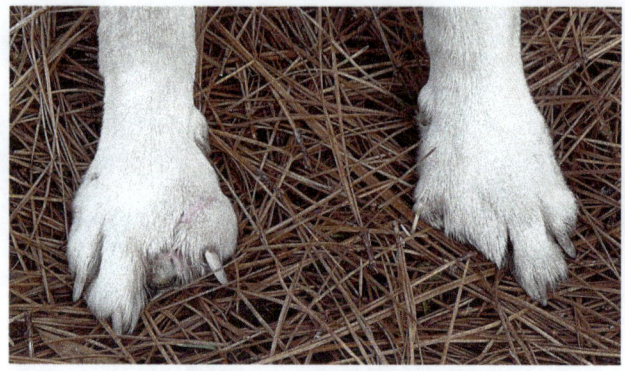

Batman's front feet when he arrived

hounds was missing toes on his front feet and had exposed flesh and bone on another foot. My first thought was that maybe he had gotten his feet hung on something? Maybe even a trap? Sadly, upon closer examination, we discovered one foot had the toes cut off in a straight line, probably by shears or something similar. The other foot was not quite as clean a cut as the first. I am guessing by the second foot the dog was thrashing, biting, and trying to get away. We were horrified to think of how this could

Batman loved cuddles with the volunteers.

have happened… After our vet examined him, she too, felt that his toes were purposely cut. We discovered once we put them in a temporary holding area that, even with missing, sore toes, the one dog was able to climb out. Thankfully, he did not run away, but that incident did give us insight as to why someone, as cruel as it was, decided to cut off his toes. They probably thought this would keep him from climbing out.

We came to call this duo Batman and Robin, since that seemed appropriate for the pair that were willing to stick together, even if it meant they would starve together. Batman is the dog whose toes were cut. There was not anything medically that could be done to help him but keep his feet clean, so that his feet would heal without risk for infection. Batman and Robin got their checkups and shots, and we kept them on a steady diet. Pretty soon, they were both at good weights and seemed to be more independent, so we proceeded to adopt Robin out to one of our

Batman, after gaining some much needed weight, out for a walk with SC CARES co-founder Skip.

volunteers who still shares his companionship. Batman ended up in the house with us, and blended in nicely with the other six canines that lived with us.

This poor boy has a terminal limp and recently, after having x-rays, we discovered that his back leg had been

Batman loves laying on a lap, pictured with Cindy.

fractured at some point in his life, in addition to everything else he had been through. Our best guess was that he had been hit by a car. He is our gimpy boy who loves to love us. When he is on the couch with us, he has to be either laying on you or at least touching you.

How can a creature that has been so tortured by humans ever trust a human again? Even several years later, when I picture in my thoughts how this tragedy occurred for him, it makes me feel nauseous and brings me to tears. Two things need to happen in our society: 1 – Hounds and all animals should be recognized as sentient creatures, not property; and 2 – Enforceable laws need to be enacted so that evil humans are not able to abuse these poor creatures without repercussions. I feel I need to be a voice for the animals, so here goes: If you cannot take on an animal as a companion and treat that being like family, then just do not have them, because to them, you are their family!!

Here in South Carolina, the animal cruelty laws are very lax. South Carolina is one of the few states remaining that allows hunting with dogs. This practice, in the eyes of animal lovers, is just barbaric! I was told by hunters that I have met through the years that they starve the dogs prior to a hunt, so that they will be more aggressive in chasing the prey. Most hunters do not spend a

Batman and his sister Lillie hanging out on the couch.

lot of money on these dogs, so they are not given medical attention of any sort. At SC CARES, we received many calls of animal cruelty, such as dogs stacked in cages, dogs tied out with no shelter, food or water. The pickup trucks that I have seen over the years with metal boxes in the back, where they cram 4-5 hunting dogs in one small crate, has simply been heartbreaking. Upon my initial investigation into animal cruelty laws in SC, I discovered that the statutes state that hounds used for hunting are considered property and not covered under ANY animal cruelty laws. So, basically, they can be treated in any manner and nothing can be done about it! This is such an incredibly sad situation. Let me say that I am sure this does not apply to all hunters. There are probably some that care for their dogs, but honestly, the practice of hunting with dogs, hunting at all, breaks the heart of an animal lover.

Over the years, Skip and I personally took in at least a dozen hunting hounds, and every single one that showed up on our doorstep was emaciated, full of fleas and ticks, heartworm positive, and some with Lyme disease. Treatment to heal them costs thousands of dollars, but to see them later stretched out on the couch, healthy and happy, was worth it all! They all ended up in our tiny house, and at one time, there were nine dogs living with us in our 900 square foot house! Yes, I know it is crazy, but it's all worth it in the end! Animals are amazing in their ability to forgive humans and know that not all of us are alike!

Batman's crazy sleeping positions.

A couch full of love.

Gracie, our 16-year-old glider.

5
Grace, the Sugar Glider

Grace was a sugar glider that was rescued from a breeding mill in California. These adorable little creatures are bred in situations, much like "puppy mills," to be sold in pet stores across the nation. Even before the beginning of SC CARES, we started taking in animals that had nowhere to go, and Grace and three of her friends were among those we moved to South Carolina with us. A breeding mill was raided and ordered to be shut down. Animal Control had made a decision to euthanize the gliders. A fellow rescuer purchased an airline ticket, flew to California, and brought back four of the gliders set to be put down. Gracie, Will, Bob and Sherrie came to live with us. Sugar gliders normally live 8-12 years in captivity and at 16 years old, she outlived her entire group.

There are breeders selling the infant joeys (joeys are what baby gliders are called, just like kangaroos and opossums) to make a profit. We have turned away gliders that we did not have room for, and currently there are sugar gliders on petfinder.com that are up for adoption. These breeders market them as "Sugar Bears" or "Pocket Pets," which makes them even more appealing. What they may not emphasize is that they are nocturnal and prefer to sleep during the day; they do have a musky smell naturally; can be messy to clean up behind, and should live for at least 8-12 years. Most people get tired of them way before their lifespan is over, and sadly, there are not enough sanctuaries to take them all.

Squirt, Gracie's roommate, and one of her neighbors (below).

Sugar gliders are remarkably like our flying squirrels found here on the North American continent, but these little babes are in the wild in Australia. Sugar gliders are marsupials, which means females

Gracie, the Sugar Glider

have a pouch in which to carry their young, like kangaroos, koalas, and opossums. They also have a prehensile tail (meaning their tails can grasp or hold) which would allow them to hold onto branches like primates do when moving through treetops. Creatures that live in trees are called arboreal. Sugar gliders are very social creatures and, in the wild, live in colonies where they share finding food and watching for predators, such as owls, snakes and feral cats. Gliders are omnivores, which means they eat plants and animals. In the wild, one of their favorite things is eucalyptus leaves, but they would also eat nectar, seeds, bird eggs, fungi (mushrooms), fruits, and bugs of all sorts. Here at SC CARES our gliders received a variety of foods including pellets (formulated especially for glider nutrition), cereal mix, all sorts of fruits and veggies, plus mealworms, which they really love! Every Sunday, we give them yogurt drops (also formulated for gliders), giving them a calcium boost. They gobble them up and who could blame them, the drops smell like cake batter – umm good! Below, enjoying fruits and veggies.

Sugar gliders, being arboreal and living in the treetops, are very agile at getting around. This is due in part to a flap of skin between the front and back legs called a patagium. They cannot technically fly but, when they stretch their legs out while jumping, the patagium extends and looks like a hang glider giving them the effects of flying, as well as their name. When they launch themselves from one tree to another, the patagium enables them to glide 150 feet or more. They do all of these acrobatic feats in the dark, being nocturnal they sleep during the day and are active at night. Their large eyes give them the ability to see better with little or no light. They are amazing creatures and should not be held captive for human entertainment, but instead live their lives free in the wild!

Snuggling in for bed time (daytime for us).

Norman as a baby.

6
Two Cows, One Moo

Meet Norman, an Angus steer who came to SC CARES at just 6 months of age. Angus is a breed of cow, and steer means male. Norman was born on a local farm where cows were raised to be sold for meat at auction. Thankfully, due to a very strange occurrence, this would not be Norman's fate! Apparently, donkeys are often kept in fields as a protector for cows. Donkeys are very fierce, when it comes to protecting the herd, and will even take on a coyote if they are a threat! For whatever the reason, this donkey decided to grab Norman by his back leg and drag him across the field, breaking his leg in the process.

The farmer attempted to set his leg (improperly though and with no pain medication), and then he put Norman in a stall by himself. The farmer tried to feed him, but it was not nearly enough, and Norman never saw his mom again nor was he able to nurse from her.

After several months Norman had reached 6 months of age but was very stunted, because he did not get enough to eat. His broken leg had healed in a crooked, stiff position. The farmer knew he would not get any money for him, so he decided he would put him down. A young man who helped the farmer knew of SC CARES, and thankfully, his heart felt bad for Norman, so he convinced the farmer to let us have him! As soon as Norman arrived, we called the vet to get an appointment to have him checked.

We had to transport Norman to the vet about 30 miles away, and the only vehicle we had was a van. The back seats had been removed, so we had room for Norman to ride in the back. Even though stunted, he still weighed well over 100 pounds, but Skip and I hoisted him into the van, and I decided to ride in the back with him to try to keep him calm and still. We made it to the vet's office without incident, and they came out to help us get him inside. They radiographed (x-rayed) his leg and discovered the farmer had set it crooked. By now the bones had calcified in this position, and the only way to correct it would be to send him to the Vets School in Georgia so they could re-break it, re-set it, and hope that it would heal properly. The success rate for this was extremely low, on top of the $8,000 cost! The vet's diagnosis was that, since the leg had calcified and Norman used it to stand and move about without showing any signs of pain, he felt that Norman would be okay with his leg like this, if he continued to use it and if we kept his weight from becoming too heavy. So, we decided to do nothing and keep an eye on him as he grew.

Now for the ride home! On our way back to the sanctuary, Norman's body decided he had to poo! I am still sitting in the back with him, and he started trying to stand up! I tried to work with him to get him to lay back down, but little did I know that he was standing up to poo! Well, let me tell you, it was quite a sight when we arrived back to the sanctuary. Skip opened the back of van and there I was with Norman and poo everywhere, even in my purse! After getting Norman out and settled, the clean up began. Eventually, we got everything cleaned up and sanitized! I am quite sure traveling with a 6-month-old calf in the back of a van was not the brightest idea, but thankfully, we all made it!

Norman grew as we fed him cow chow, beet pulp and sweet feed and, of course, his hay, which he loved! We kept an eye on his weight. Years went by and Norman continued to use his leg. As fate would have it, Norman's body adjusted to his disability, and his good leg had grown to twice the size of the broken one and was very muscular to help carry his weight. Norman had free run of our entire back yard area, where people would walk around for tours, as well as our volunteers as we fed the other animals. Norman started to get frisky and began to chase people. It was quite funny to see him chasing people, but not so funny when you are the one being chased! All you could do was get behind a tree and play peek-a-boo until he got bored, or someone came to distract him. Norman would put both of his back legs together when he ran, and he was able to run faster than you would expect! To keep everyone safe, we gated Norman off in his own area, still with plenty of room but not where people were moving about.

Norman loving his hay!

Norman was the spokesman for all the animals when it was time to eat, and his internal clock was on the mark! He would "MOO" and bellow out non-stop, until we started feeding everyone. You could hear Norman "MOOING" all over the sanctuary!

Several years after Norman's arrival, we were asked

Above, Norman with a bald patch on his forehead.

Below, the reason Norman has a bald patch – his scratching post!

Mayflower resting and looking regal!

to take in another cow who was all by herself at a neighboring sanctuary. Introducing Mayflower, a Charolais Bovine heifer! Charolais is a breed of cow, bovine is the technical name for cow, and heifer means female. Mayflower had a terrible beginning to life, and I will not go into specifics in this story, but she was discarded and not allowed to be with her mom either. The difference in Mayflower and Norman's situation is like night and day though! Where Norman was stuck in a stall without much care or feeding at all, Mayflower was loved, and bottle-fed by her new human friends. Those at the sanctuary caring for her fed her as much as her natural mom would have, so she got plenty to eat and grew … and grew! However, Mayflower was the only cow that lived there, the other animals were mainly pigs.

Mayflower was given the absolute best care and after two years had grown into the beautiful girl that she is

Chewing on a pine branch!

Don't you want a kiss??

today! There was one big downside to all this though, Mayflower was imprinted, meaning she had no idea at all that she was a huge 1600-pound cow! She played like she was a 10-pound puppy, but when Mayflower ran, you could feel the ground shaking, so it was hugely different from a puppy!

Mayflower never "MOOED"! She really did not

Coming to see you!

make any sounds at all! This is the result of not being raised around other cows and being imprinted to humans. When she got excited, she would start running and kicking her back legs up in the air, and at times, she would even stand up on her back legs towering over any scrawny human! Unlike horses who can only kick backwards, cows can also kick to the side as well! Not to mention that they can use their heads to move things around, namely ME! Once when I went in to feed her, Mayflower took her head and aimed right at my stomach and lifted me off the ground! I will admit I was terrified that she was going to knock me down and step on me which would not have been good. It took me several minutes to stop shaking, once I was out of there. To her, she was simply playing, but because I was not a

Both cows waiting for a treat!

1600-pound cow that could play back, she could have surely brought me to my end!

We knew that with Mayflower's size and Norman being stunted and crippled, these two cows could not be put together in the same area, since Norman would most likely get hurt. Since cows are very social creatures and used to being part of a herd, Norman and Mayflower made the best of it and would lay together at the fence, almost touching, so I think this brought them both comfort. Although Mayflower did not "MOO," Norman made up for it with his loud bellows of "MOOING"!

On a side note, people would often ask us if we milked Mayflower. So many were unaware that only when a cow is pregnant does her body produce milk! Just like human women, after all, cows and people are both mammals!

Monte loving on one of our volunteers!

7
Monte – Please Don't Skip This Story

I know that many people are terrified of snakes and honestly, I used to be, too! In other stories, you have heard how important all animals are to their environment; well, the snakes are important, too! I have attempted to cover some information that may give you a little insight as to just what a snake's purpose is, and I hope that it will help you feel a bit better about them.

Before I even start this story, I want to make it clear that all snakes are better left alone, especially those in the wild, since some of them are venomous and harmful to us as humans. As a note, people often say that a snake is poisonous, but that's incorrect, because poisonous means that just touching them would give you their poison! For snakes, this is not the case. There are poisonous frogs, caterpillars, and other animals whose poison is absorbed simply by touching them, but a snake's venom must be injected. For that reason they are referred to as venomous, like scorpions and some spiders.

The ecosystem is an extremely delicate and complicated arrangement. If the scales are tilted too far in any direction, it could bring chaos to the entire system, a system in which we also exist. We have all heard of the food chain where there are predators that eat certain animals. If all the predators are extinguished, then the animals that they eat would certainly overpopulate. Snakes everywhere eat small animals, such as mice and rats, in addition to other creatures. Snakes and other predators are responsible for keeping those populations in check, so that the earth is not overrun with too many of them. An overpopulation of one species of animal could bring great harm to us as humans, as it did from 1346 until 1353 when the bubonic plague killed millions of people. This plague was said to be caused by an overpopulation of rats and fleas. These animals are also an important species when their numbers are kept in balance.

Trying to be sneaky!.

Meet Monte, the ball python, who would normally live in the wild in Africa. Monte and many other species of snakes from other countries have been introduced by the pet industry and

Such a sweet boy!

are being sold everywhere as pets. Of course, my belief is that all wild animals should be allowed to remain just that – "wild." Monte was someone's pet and, for whatever reason, ended up outside in North Carolina. We are not sure whether he escaped his previous home or was simply put out because his owners no longer wanted him. Monte was found near another house, and the people who lived there were not educated about snakes. Like so many others, they did not realize he was not venomous but was

This action is called telescoping!

a constrictor, meaning he squeezes his prey. In their horror, seeing this 3-foot-long large snake, they got a golf club and began to hit him over the head. Thankfully, someone nearby stopped them and called animal control officers, and they were able to catch him. They then called the wildlife hotline, and Monte was taken in.

Monte's injuries were treated and eventually he healed, although he bears the scar on his head from his near-death experience.

Monte coming out to meet a new friend! Notice the scar right on top of his head.

Monte came to live at SC CARES, even before SC CARES was formed. I have grown to love him and love holding him. Unlike what a lot of people think, he is neither cold nor slimy but instead is a warm body of muscle that loves to wrap around your arm and take a ride. He also loves being held in a ball like a baby, hence the

Monte's hand cuddle!

name "ball" python. Monte was such an important ambassador for us! SO many people who came for tours were initially terrified, but after touching and gently petting him, they grew to feel so comfortable that many asked to hold all three feet of him! It was such a thrill to witness this transition take place and in only a few minutes!

Monte really enjoys going outside to sit in the sun and sometimes getting down to slink across the grass. When Monte is in the sun, he has the most beautiful iridescent coloring all over his entire body.

Enjoying his time in the grass!

We would give Monte a bath quite often, since snakes shed every couple of months, but due to Monte's scar, he has a tougher time shedding. Snakes usually shed from the head all the way down to the tail and a healthy shed will come off all in one piece, much like a rolled-up sock. Monte's scar kept his skin from shedding off like it should, so we would run a warm bath for him in the sink and rub his body until we got all the skin off. When snakes shed, they also have a blue colored "eye cap" over each of their eyes that looks just like a contact lens!

Monte is alive and well as of 2021 and, hopefully, will continue to be happy for years to come, thanks to one of our dedicated volunteers who adopted him. The ball python's life span can be up to 30 years, but we have

Hiding in his log!

no idea what his true age might be, since he was found as an adult. I have known him for 17 years, so maybe he has a long time left to be alive on this earth. I realize this story may not convince you to love snakes, but my hope is that you would at least consider respecting the snakes of our world, since they are also important in the ecosystem we share!

8
Kumar

Kumar came to SC CARES in 2008 at two years of age. We received a call from a rescuer who had taken in a llama that she could no longer keep. The llama kept charging her when she entered his pasture area. Originally, we thought he could live with the two horses we had rescued at that time, but the horses thought otherwise. Kumar is a beautiful animal but had a few quirks. His history tells us that he had been taken away from his mom and his herd, then bottle-fed by humans. He lived in the house with the humans, sleeping on the bed and laying around with people. It sounds adorable, right? Not so good for the llama, though. Due to this handling in his beginning stages of life, he developed what is called

"Berserk Llama Syndrome," meaning crazy llama! I am not joking! This is a psychological disorder found to be potentially extremely dangerous for those working with him. Extensive studies have been done on this issue and the conclusion is that this disorder occurs primarily in males as a result of over-bonding with humans, instead of being raised with their moms and their herd, which is their true family. Once Kumar had gotten too large to stay in the house (and, I imagine, the poop became too much as well), he was tethered and tied outside with a dog collar around his neck. This did not go over well with the llama who thought he was human, and who could blame him?

Many of the llamas that have endured this imprinting and isolation from other llamas and have developed "berserk llama syndrome," usually become so aggressive to humans that they are nearly impossible to keep. So many are so angry that they break down fences to attack humans and end up being put down. I suppose in Kumar's case, we were extremely lucky in that he did not go to those efforts to

This is what Kumar looked like when he arrived, notice the dog collar.

attack; he generally just did not tolerate us – especially in his area. Llamas in general are very territorial by nature. We considered finding a friend for Kumar and, in the interim, tried one of our larger goats to be a companion for him, but that did not work out. Kumar was not happy about having another creature live with him, so we decided that taking in another llama might not turn out so well, either.

Llamas have various means of defense. Spitting is their first line of attack. Although it is not painful, it can be very unpleasant and is meant as a warning to say "I am not happy – leave me alone." There are three levels of spitting: the first from the mouth is a little smelly but not too bad. Next is the esophageal spit, which takes a minute to work up and is even more "fragrant" than the mouth spit. Finally, there is the stomach spit, said to be comparable to being sprayed by a skunk. Thankfully, Kumar never got this upset with us, but of course, we tried really hard not to aggravate him, either. Their necks are all muscle, and they use them to try to knock the offender down to the ground. Once on the ground, they stomp and kick and, weighing 250 pounds, they could easily do damage. Llamas also have fighting teeth, used of course for biting.

Llamas are part of the camelid family, originating from Peru. Their larger cousins are the camels, and the smaller cousins are the alpacas. All these creatures are known as pack animals and have been used for centuries to carry goods in travel. Llamas are said to be able to carry 25-30% of their body weight. Kumar weighed 250 pounds

Kumar before shearing.

but male llamas can weigh anywhere from 225-450 pounds, so needless to say these animals are extraordinarily strong! There are people who herd llamas for their wool; after shearing them, they spin the wool to make garments like sweaters.

Kumar getting a hair cut and yes, it was quite an ordeal!

Kumar after shearing.

Kumar investigating the pool we got for him to cool off in.

Llamas, like horses, use their ears to communicate. If the ears are upright and forward, it means he is curious and may want attention, but if those ears lay back, watch out! That is a sign of displeasure and the spit might be next!! It was interesting to watch him interact with people; sometimes, he would become defensive right away, and other times, he really seemed to enjoy himself.

From his curious look, "I might like you?"

To "I don't think so!" and then ...
the face you DO NOT want to see!!

Kumar is about to spit!

He was not particularly fond of men, any man, but some women were able to pet him, and a few even gave him a kiss! Animals are highly intelligent creatures and often we do not give them the credit they deserve. Kumar may have trusted scent to judge people, but I also think that he was intuitive, meaning he could sense automatically whether or not he liked someone. Kumar was definitely one of our popular creatures to visit when people came out for tours, and if you were one of the "lucky" ones he spit on, then your visit was even more memorable!

One of the lucky women getting a kiss. Look at those happy ears!

Kumar

Meet Pickles!

Meet Handsome!

10
Pickles & Handsome, Demolition Duo

In this story you will find out just how destructive parrots can be! Meet Pickles, a female African Grey, and do not let her funny name fool you, this bird is highly intelligent! Pickles came to us along with a friend, an Amazon named Harry, after the death of their human owner. It took Pickles quite a while to adjust to her new life and her new home but when she finally did, she was hilarious! Her previous human must have spent a great deal of time with these birds, since Pickles had a lengthy vocabulary, but her friend Harry never said a word.

Pickles was amazing as she began to share her previous world with us. She would sing "Shake, shake, shake; Shake, shake, shake; shake your booty, shake your booty" by KC & the Sunshine Band, and did this in tune, I might add! She also sang another song or at least started it and that was, "Take me out to the ballgame…" By not finishing it, the humans who were in the hut would sing it for her! Pickles' human must have had a bird feeder right

Pickles in her defensive mode.

outside their window, since Pickles would fuss at the squirrels saying, "BAD squirrel," and she would say this in a disapproving tone. Pickles lived on a golf course and one of the funniest phrases was yelling, "Say fore, use the nine iron!" While she lived at the sanctuary, she learned to say "Merry Christmas" which was funny to hear in July! Of course, like you might expect a lot of parrots would do, she would say "Pretty Bird" and of course we would answer with "Yes, you are!"

Aside from her amusing phrases, Pickles was also bilingual! Yes, you read it right, she could speak in several other languages! In French, "Parlez-vous français?" meaning "Do you speak French?" Then in German "Sprechen Sie Deutsch" which translates to "Do you speak German?" Then finally in Spanish "Que pasa, Julio?" meaning "What's up, Julio?" Knowing so many different languages and speaking so many other words, we knew that Pickles' former human spent a lot of time and attention with her birds, which is heartwarming, as many of our parrots were not that fortunate.

At SC CARES we were able to let nearly all of the birds out to play during the day, after breakfast. This brings me to introduce you to Handsome, a male African Grey that had come to live at SC CARES only a year after we had opened. Handsome came to us from a breeder nearby that thankfully shut down his operation and asked us to take his birds, all 18 of them! It was a lot to take on at once but, fortunately, we had the space since we had just started our rescue.

Handsome had been quiet and kept to himself most of time. The only thing we were able to teach him to say was "Handsome boy." Parrots, like people, all have different personalities. Some are outgoing and love to talk and interact, while others

Handsome looking regal!

may be a little shy and keep more to themselves. Also, like people, they tend to pair up with their opposites. Now, at the time Pickles arrived, Handsome lived in the front of the hut and Pickles near the back, so they really did not see each other, but I am sure Handsome could hear Pickles! I do not recall exactly when it occurred, but one day Handsome flew to the back and met Pickles! From that point on, these two were together every single day!

In the hut, there was an upper and lower row of cabinets against one of the walls. The upper cabinet had about a foot of space above it, and that is where these two could usually be found! As I have mentioned in other stories about parrots, they need lots of stimulation or toys to chew on and play with. We noticed Pickles and Handsome had starting chewing on the wall above the upper cabinets, so we placed what we thought were exciting toys on the cabinet and the counter below. The demolition duo was more interested in chewing on everything else! I need to mention that they did not eat any of this, they just chewed it all into tiny pieces. These two were quiet while doing this and, to be honest, we often forgot about it as there was so much going on and other

Pickles again, notice the hard board behind her!

birds flying about. As it turns out, they not only chewed through the sheetrock of the wall but also chewed several holes in the cabinet below!

Skip placed heavy duty boards across the wall so the birds would not accidently fall through the hole they had accomplished and end up in the middle of the wall! Once the boards were in place, they found it more difficult to chew on them, so they ventured down to the counter below.

Pickles daring you to reach up to her!

We stored items on the counter, including any surplus of apples that had been donated. Pickles and Handsome decided to go under the towel that covered the apples and have a snack. We love for our animals to have treats, so I put an entire apple out on the counter for them to eat or chew on. When I returned a few minutes later,

Pickles (inside the box) and Handsome (on the side) playing in a box we gave them in an attempt to keep them from tearing down more of the wall behind them.

Another play box and time for a treat!

the apple was still there, just as I had left it, and Pickles and Handsome were under the towel taking bites out of every single apple in the bin! What a mess!

Pickles and Handsome, like all the other parrots, need stimulation, something to do. They are not satisfied just sitting and watching the world go by, they want to be part of it, too! No different than people, they need projects, things to do and be excited about! We all enjoy being a part of our world and not just in it!

Mother and son out exploring their new home.

11
A Mother and Son

SC CARES received a call to take in an elderly female goat, so Skip and I went to pick her up. When we arrived, there were SO many goats, maybe 30 or more, all living at this man's house. The man led us to a goat he called Grandma. He said he named her that because she had given birth to so many babies. Grandma goat had an open sore on her cheek, and the man explained how she would get these spots on her cheek that would rupture and look infected, but he would clean it, put salve on it and eventually it would heal. We asked if a vet had checked it, but he said no that this had happened to other goats and it always healed up. Of course, Skip and I would call our vets as soon as we returned!

"Grandma" – notice the knot on the side of her face.

So, we started leading Grandma to our vehicle. As we got away from the herd, a cute little boy started baying out and following us to our vehicle. It was a heart-wrenching cry! This little one did not want his mom to leave! The other goats seemed unaffected but not this little fella, and with his cries of anguish, I had already decided I was not leaving him! The man tried to get the little goat back to the herd, but this sweet boy was incredibly determined! Finally, the man asked if we wanted him, too, and of course I said ABSOLUTELY!

Once we returned to SC CARES, we unloaded the two goats to a temporary pen and called the vet. Thankfully, he was able to come out that day. He examined them both and the place on Grandma's cheek and drew some blood for testing. The vet said he was sure Grandma had CASEOUS LYMPHADENITIS (CL). This is a highly

Jackson as a baby when we met him.

contagious disease affecting the lymph node system. Goats with CL will have abscesses appear under the skin that rupture, opening to release the fluids, which is what is highly contagious. After bloodwork results confirmed the vet's suspicion, he did surgery to remove the abscess, but it was unsuccessful, and the nasty, huge pimple appeared again a couple of months later. Sadly, this disease was passed at birth to ALL the goats that Grandma had given birth to which, according to the man, was a lot! This is a perfect example of humans being irresponsible with animals, and not giving them the medical care they deserve or doing all he could to prevent it from spreading. There is no excuse for this careless and uncaring action! There is now a vaccine for this, but it has not been proven to be completely successful and carries some serious side effects. Currently there is no cure for CL.

Above, Grandma hiding from us after her surgery, notice the stitches on the left side of her face.

Below, Jackson laying with his momma after her surgery, notice the stitches on the right side of her face.

Meanwhile, she and her son, who we named Jackson, lived separately from all the other animals. Grandma was so sweet and would allow us to pet her, but Jackson was very shy and would not have anything to do with us. Honestly, who could blame him? Humans separated him from his herd which was his family, so why wouldn't he think that humans were bad? We had to be careful when we left them and wash our hands, so we would not pass this disease on to the other animals.

Mother and Son

Grandma the day she arrived.

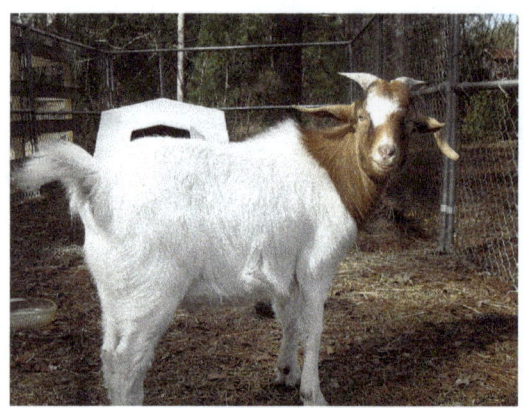

Jackson in their temporary area.

Can we come out and play?!

Love at First Sight

We built a nice area with a great house for Grandma and Jackson and away from other animals. They really seemed to enjoy it! As Jackson grew, he became somewhat of a twit, trying to eat his food and Grandma's, too! Since Grandma had jumped to the top of their house before, we decided to build a ramp so she could access it daily. Jackson had never tried to get up there, so we started feeding Grandma on the roof where she could eat in peace! The only time this was a problem was when it was raining. If you know anything about goats, you will know that most of them hate to get wet! All our goats would run into their houses if it started raining. It was really kind of funny and reminded me of women with a new hairdo not wanting it to get wet! Therefore, on rainy days we had to feed them inside their houses, and hopefully Grandma stood her ground with Jackson. Her consistent weight led us to know she did!

The mother and son duo seemed happy together and, after breakfast, were let out into an extremely large area to explore. Grandma was 16 years old when she came to SC CARES, but do not let her age fool you, when it was time to eat, she would jump to the roof of her house and bay out to let you know she was ready!

Grandma taking it easy. Such a beautiful ole girl!

Mother and Son

12
Chester, the One-Eyed Owl

Chester is a magnificent creature with tremendous strength and yet graceful at the same time. The Great Horned Owl is the largest owl in our area. They are mighty hunters of the night, using sound triangulation to pinpoint exactly where their prey is located, along with great binocular vision in dim lighting which gives them a great advantage in finding food. The owl's eyes are exceptionally large compared to the eyes we have, therefore, they are not able to move their eyes from side to side like humans, but can rotate their heads 270 degrees giving

Standing tall but get a look at those talons!

them full view from all sides of their bodies. Their hearing is impeccable; their ears are not directly across from each other, they are located one higher and forward and the other lower and back farther on the head, thus giving them remarkable accuracy in depth perception and location with just a tilt of the head. Many people think the "horns" on their head are their ears, but actually they are not ears or horns, simply a group of feathers the owl can raise or lower.

Their beaks are intimidating, but watch out for those talons! With a gripping potential of 300 psi (pounds of pressure per square inch), the Great Horned Owl in most cases kills its prey instantly upon capture. For those not familiar with this type of strength, let me say that it only takes about 200 psi to break most of the bones in the human body, so those very sharp talons mixed with such brute force – well, you can imagine the damage they could inflict! Even the strongest human could not get the force of 300 psi in their grip.

Chester is a Raptor Bird of Prey – the term "raptor" means to kill with their feet and also includes hawks, falcons, eagles, etc. Another wonder of the owl is the way their feathers are constructed, with what is called shoots and barbs and a fluffy, downy edge. The way the feathers are arranged gives them silent flight. They are the only raptors with feathering on their legs and feet as well. In one of our wildlife classes, the teacher presented the wing of a hawk and the wing of an owl for us to inspect. They both looked the same to us. Then, we were asked to close our eyes and listen, we heard a swishing sound as that of a wing moving through the air, then we heard nothing... the silence was the wing of the owl. This is a particularly good tool for the owl since, being nocturnal, they hunt at night and generally our environment is quieter then. It gives them a little more of an advantage to be successful in finding food.

Great Horned Owls feed on small mammals, such as mice, rats, rabbits, squirrels, and they will even eat other birds. When the balance of life is not disturbed, all our

Inside Chester's house, notice his handicap ramp so that he can climb to his perch just in case he is not able to fly to it!

predator/prey creatures keep species numbers in check. When that balance is disturbed, things seem to go awry... such as what some say is now an over-population of deer, due to fact that humans have killed or removed the deer's predators. Life is all about balance not only for us as humans but also for the delicate eco-system we live in.

All raptors are protected and governed by US Fish & Wildlife, a Federal Agency within the Department of Interior. It is illegal to possess a raptor, even a feather of a raptor. For us to be able to have Chester at SC CARES, we had to attend classes and intern with the Carolina Raptor Center in North Carolina. Then we had to build his enclosure and send a lengthy application, with references, to apply for a permit for him to be a part of our education program. When a raptor is found injured, it should be taken to a center that can handle the injuries and determine the probability of releasing the creature back to its wild home. Locally, we are fortunate to have a wonderful raptor center nearby – Center for Birds of Prey – located in Awendaw. If for any reason a raptor cannot be released, it must be placed in an educational program with the proper permits or euthanasia is the only other option. They cannot be kept as pets.

Outside of Chester's house.

Chester came to us after being hit by a car which caused him to lose sight in his left eye, which is why it looks different. Chester was in the care of our former wildlife group in North Carolina. Under veterinarian care, it was determined that Chester not only had the eye injury but also damage to his rotator cuff which is why he could not be released. In his flight test, he was unable to gain altitude in flight due to his shoulder injury, which would be detrimental to his survival in the wild. Therefore, Chester could not be released.

Sadly, our society has created an atmosphere for

the raptor/vehicle collisions to occur more frequently by clearing roads and even placing poles (perches for them) along the path. Thankfully, our society has taken a much-needed stand on litter but there are those who still think it is all right to throw garbage from their cars. Even organic matter such as apple cores or banana peels are items that attract the little creatures that the raptors hunt for food, thus causing risk of being hit by oncoming traffic. These stealthy hunters are so attuned to the movements of their prey that they are not even aware of vehicles, which is why they are hit.

Chester watching the sun come up which in his case means "Good night!"

9
The Sweetest Family Ever!

Allow me to introduce you to one of the sweetest families you could ever meet – SC CARES wolf hybrids! This wolf hybrid pack quickly became one of our most popular groups! They all loved attention and were just as willing to give attention in return. This hybrid family came to SC CARES from a lady who had fought extremely hard to keep them. Sadly, her neighbor would irritate these animals at the fence, then call the police for all the barking. The poor lady ended up in court over this, and the judge told her to place the animals somewhere else; otherwise, if she were back in her courtroom again, the lady would go to jail and the animals would be euthanized! Thankfully, we were able to take them in.

The lady who had them originally said the male had wolf in his lineage, and before she knew it, he and the female had mated and had pups! With wolf hybrids, it is often difficult to tell exactly how much wolf their bloodline may contain without doing a blood test to confirm DNA, but with this pack we are sure their percentages are high content dog. Based on information from our wolf advisor, if they can eat kibble (dog food) without stomach upset, then it is most likely they are high content dog. Also, the front leg placement is another sign; the wolves' front legs are closer together, seeming to extend from the chest and not the shoulder area. This is probably what gives wolves more speed while running. The most distinct difference is the higher the wolf content, the less likely they will bark. Wolves howl and do not bark, and this family all loved to bark!

Meet Shiloh, the only male in the family and the one with suspected wolf lineage. This may be true, but Shiloh was a sweet boy who loved to be loved! We also called him "papa," since

Shiloh, Papa dog!

The Sweetest Family Ever

Momma dog, Deja, always so beautiful!

he was the father of his two girls. His mate, Deja, was the mom to the girls and just as sweet as Shiloh! She loved to be hugged and loved giving kisses! We called her "momma dog."

Above, our first meeting!

Below, years later and always giving kisses!

Lobo – one of the daughters.

Next, we have Lobo, the one that to me looks like she should be a police dog! Lobo is for sure the first one to bark and is a bit leery of strangers. Some of our volunteers had to wait months before she would finally come close for a pet!

Last but certainly not least, we have Fuzzy, the greeter of the family! Fuzzy never met a stranger and would give hugs and kisses to anyone! Fuzzy absolutely lives up to her name and has SO much hair that we had to give her a haircut just to help her shed her winter coat! The others did well with just brushing!

A house on stilts was constructed for

Fuzzy, the greeter!

The Sweetest Family Ever

the family, so they would have shade under it to lay in on those hot days! The house had a porch with an overhang at the door and steps on both sides of the porch to get down to the ground. Skip also constructed a pool for them, not only for drinking but also big enough for them to get in and walk around to cool off. Hot days in South Carolina are even worse when you have so much hair! We also had a heater in their house for those cold winter days! I believe this family enjoyed their time with us, and we certainly enjoyed having them!

We were fortunate that this wolf hybrid pack was a high content dog family but that may not be the case for other wolf hybrids that live in family settings. There are many people breeding wolves with dogs, then selling them to others who take them into family situations. If the animal is high content wolf, it may be difficult to

All but Fuzzy in this summer family photo.

Fuzzy was staying hydrated!

domesticate them, since instincts are stronger than any training! This is not to say some people are not successful with these situations, but many cases turn out dreadful when the animal's instincts take over. These scenarios usually do not end well, especially for the animal. Just remember wolves are wild and dogs are domestic!

When I look into the eyes of an animal, I see a soul!

Afterword

All the stories in *Tails from SC CARES* and *Love at First Sight* are based on true events from the life of the sanctuary director, Cindy Hedrick, Co-founder/Co-director of SC CARES. All creatures big and small, at SC CARES we loved them all!! This book was written to give readers an idea of the amazing perseverance, gratitude and personalities of some of the many animals we met. Their stories will tell you of trials and hardships they had to overcome, and how they survived and learned to trust and love again!

The dictionary defines "animal sanctuary" as: a facility where animals are brought to live and be protected for the rest of their lives. Unlike animal shelters, sanctuaries do not seek to place animals with individuals or groups, instead maintaining each animal until his or her natural death. The mission of sanctuaries is generally to be safe havens, where the animals receive the best care that the sanctuaries can provide. Animals are not bought, sold, or traded, nor are they used for animal testing. The resident animals are given the opportunity to behave as naturally as possible in a protective environment. A sanctuary is not open to the public in the sense of a zoo; that is, the public is not allowed unescorted access to any part of the facility. A sanctuary tries not to allow any activity that would place the animals in an unduly stressful situation. One of the most important missions of sanctuaries, beyond caring for the animals, is educating the public. The ultimate goal of a sanctuary should be to change the way that humans think of, and treat, non-human animals. This definition perfectly describes what SC CARES was all about.

As the former director of an animal rescue, we are very grateful for people who care about wildlife and want to help them. If you find a creature in need of help, please contact a wildlife rehabilitation center to help them.

In the Georgetown/Horry County area:
https://wildthingsfc.org/

SC DNR has this list of rehabilitation centers: **https://www.dnr.sc.gov/wildlife/rehab/index.html.**

Too many times these creatures are orphaned, abandoned or injured, and people are trying to help but often don't realize the impact they are having by keeping the animal too long or their having too much contact with humans and other companion animals. For instance, an infant squirrel, cared for by humans possibly around dogs or cats, will not be a candidate for release if he imprints and is too used to these other creatures and not familiar with how to find food in the wild. We've received numerous calls from well-meaning people who have kept wildlife as a "pet" and, in most cases, the call comes in when the animal has reached sexual maturity. This changes the animal's attitude immensely; their instincts tell them they need to breed and in captivity that won't happen. Our hearts go out to these creatures who usually end up being put down – deer, raccoons, opossums, squirrels. They are all meant to be in the wild – even when their life expectancy is probably half what it might be in captivity. I'm sure they'd choose two years of freedom, enjoying all of the things their instincts tell them to, rather than four years in what is similar to a prison for them.

Words used in Love at First Sight and what they mean

Arboreal – animals that live in trees

Bilingual – ability to speak in two languages

Bovine – an animal in the cattle family

Camelid – a mammal in the camel family

Compassion – to be sympathetic, care for and want to help all living creatures

Constrictor – a snake that squeezes its prey

Ecosystem – a complex network of living creatures

Esophageal – refers to mucus (spit) coming from the esophagus (throat)

Euthanasia – the act of painlessly ending a life medically with drugs

Eye cap – a scale on a snake's eye to protect the eye since they don't have eyelids

Feral – refers to an animal that is wild

High content – greater degree of wolf or dog in a wolf/dog mixed breed DNA

Hybrid – being made up of two separate species

Hydrate – to drink fluids/water to add moisture to the body

Imprinting – learned behavior, often bonding to someone other than normal

Intuitive – to know things without being told or shown

Joey – a baby animal often raised in a pouch on their mother

Lyme disease – a serious disease transmitted by ticks

Marsupial – a female mammal whose body has a pouch to carry their young

Non-releasable – not able to be set free

Patagium – a flap of skin that connects from front leg to the back leg

Predator – an animal that kills and eats other animals

Preening – to groom and smooth feathers

Prehensile – to grip or wrap around and be able to hold on

Puppy mill – a place where too many dogs are being bred, usually in poor conditions

Raptors – meat-eating birds that use their strong feet with sharp talons (nails) to hunt

Rehabilitation – the process of healing and restoring the Body

Sanctuary – a place of refuge and protection

Self-mutilate – the act of causing harm or injury to oneself

Sentient – the ability to perceive or feel things; able to feel emotions and have distinct personalities

Sound triangulation – to pinpoint an exact location by using sound

Territorial – to defend an area that an animal feels is theirs from strangers

Venomous – an animal that injects a poison by biting or stinging

Sanctuaries that helped SC CARES

Wild Things – https://wildthingsfc.org/ https://www.facebook.com/wildlifefreedom1/
Hope Acres – http://www.hopeacresrescue.org
Angel Winds Sanctuary – https://www.facebook.com/Angel-Winds-Horse-Sanctuary-283703662309798/
The Pig Preserve – https://linktr.ee/thepigpreserve
Whispering Rise Farm – http://www.wrfas.org
Flip Side Sanctuary – https://linktr.ee/flip_side_sanctuary
Charlie's Harmony Sanctuary – https://www.facebook.com/Charlies-Harmony-Sanctuary-Farm-1114675092046873/
Big Oak Wolf Sanctuary – http://www.bigoakwolfsanctuary.org
Valiant Animal Rescue – http://www.ValiantAnimalRescue.org
Izzie's Pond – http://www.izziespond.org
Wild Things Preserve – https://www.facebook.com/WildThingsPreserve/
Gainesville Rabbit Rescue – http://www.gainesvillerabbitrescue.org
Metropolitan Guinea Pig Rescue – http://www.mgpr.org
Noah's Ark Animal Sanctuary – http://www.noahs-ark.org
Papayago House Rescue – http://www.papayagorescuehouse.org
Ziggy's Haven Bird Sanctuary – http://www.ziggyshaven.org
Rescue Ranch – http://www.rescueranch.com
The Oasis Sanctuary – http://www.the-oasis.org
A Helping Wing Parrot Rescue – http://www.ahelpingwing.org

Acknowledgment

Again, my sincere thanks to the CLASS Publishing team –
Linda Ketron, Editor & Publisher,
Anne Malarich, Photography Editor,
Charlene McSweeny, Graphic Designer,
D'Ann O'Donovan & Annie Pott, Copy Editors –
for bringing this dream to reality.

~CH

www.ingramcontent.com/pod-product-compliance
Lightning Source LLC
Chambersburg PA
CBHW050857240426
43673CB00008B/268